Wait and See

Dawn L. Watkins

Photographs by Suzanne R. Altizer

Library of Congress Cataloging-in-Publication Data:

Watkins, Dawn L.
   Wait and See / Dawn L. Watkins : photographs by Suzanne R. Altizer.

    Summary: Viewing animals in partial and full-page photographs tests the
reader's ability to observe and draw conclusions.
   ISBN 0-89084-576-X
    1. Science—Observations—Pictorial works—Juvenile literature.
2. Science—Methodology—Pictorial works—Juvenile literature.
3. Perception—Pictorial works—Juvenile literature.   [1. Animals—
Pictorial works.   2. Visual perception.]   I. Altizer, Suzanne R.
(Suzanne Ramsey), 1963-   ill.   II. Title
Q163.W297   1991   91-7891
507.2—dc20   CIP
                                                  AC

Wait and See

Edited by Anne Smith

©1991 Bob Jones University Press
Greenville, South Carolina 29614

Printed in the United States of America

ISBN 0-89084-576-X

20 19 18 17 16 15 14 13 12 11 10 9 8 7 6

for
Stephen and
Matthew

DLW

for my
father,

Wade K.
Ramsey

SRA

Don't look too *fast;*
Don't look too small;
Don't think you see,
'Til you see **all**.

This could be a *bonnet*
For an Indian's head,
Or it might be the tip . . .

Of a wing widespread.

Tire of a t●y truck
●r a three-wheel bike
Is what the green c●il . . .

Of a green **S**nake is like.

This could be a grape
Or a plum turning blue,
Or it could be something . . .

That's looking at you.

Is this new carpet
That someone laid here?
Or did we just get . . .

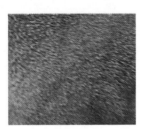

Too  to a deer?

A row of icicles
Melting in the sun

Might be nothing more . . .

Than a seal having **F** U *n.*

A teddy bear's ear
Or the top of its head
Could turn out to be . . .

A flamingo instead.

A dark brown eye
And a brow like straw
Are really the side . . .

Of a big monkey paw.

On a mountainside
Is the mouth of a cave,
But who explores here . . .

Had better be **BRAVE!**

What's at the top
Of two ~~banded~~ trees?
Not what you think . . .

Because they are knees.

An elephant's trunk
Is an elephant's nose,
And there's nothing else . . .

It can be, I suppose.

When God shows just
One part to me,
It's always best
To wait and see.

Publisher's Note

We have all had the experience of jumping to a conclusion or making a judgment with too little evidence. How much better it is to wait until we have more information; until–as the phrase goes–we have seen ''the whole picture.''

Wait and See is a visual demonstration of how a small amount of information can present a view of things that is far different from the picture revealed by the complete information. Alternate pages in the book show a section of a photograph that is out of context, accompanied by a rhyme that suggests possible interpretations to the reader. On the next page he finds the entire photograph and the last line of the rhyme, which sets things right.

The photographs and the element of surprise will invite the young reader to the book, and the accompanying rhymes can provide the reader with a basis for wide-ranging discussions. The experience of assuming one idea and discovering another may help the reader to learn that first guesses are not always accurate.

Books by Dawn L. Watkins
Medallion
Jenny Wren
A King for Brass Cobweb
The Cranky Blue Crab
Very Like a Star
Wait and See